Hitherto

Terese Adams · Holly McCullagh

First published by Busybird Publishing 2025

Copyright © 2025 Holly McCullagh, Terese Adams

ISBN: Hardcover: 978-1-923501-27-0
Ebook: 978-1-923501-28-7

This book is copyright. Apart from any fair dealing for the purposes of study, research, criticism, review, or as otherwise permitted under the Copyright Act, no part may be reproduced by any process without written permission. Enquiries should be made through the publisher.

This is a work of fiction. Any similarities between places and characters are a coincidence.

Cover image: Terese Adams

Cover design: Terese Adams

Layout and typesetting: Busybird Publishing

Editor: Krystal Herdy

Busybird Publishing
2/118 Para Road
Montmorency, Victoria
Australia 3094
www.busybird.com.au

For the girl who saved me:
Thank you for encouraging me to put my art into the world
—but more importantly, for doing it with me.

I love you more than any words I could put into a poem
could ever convey.

- T

You waltzed into my life and turned a lifelong dream into reality,
all while honouring every other dream I chase in my
pursuit of a fulfilling life.

I love you more than you will ever know.

- H

Trigger Warning:
This book contains poetry that explores themes of mental health, trauma, loss, and intense emotional experiences. Some pieces may include explicit language or be distressing to read. Reader discretion is advised.

The Reason

- The Reason -

It's her I can thank
for the kindness I have known—
a seed nurtured and quietly grown.

It incubated in the atrium of her heart,
cost her the strength she carried from the start.

Pumped out through her body,
left ventricle expands
to flow through her veins
and into her hands.

On the day I was born,
she passed it gently into mine
when she held me close
for the very first time.

Love is all I've ever known.

- The Reason -

I had a fifty percent chance
of getting it right.

And even if I did,
I'd still be half wrong.

- The Reason -

I think of who I could have been
if the child in me was not destroyed,
if I wasn't shown the harshness of the world
before my heart was ready to understand it,
but I can't imagine another life,
or another me,
that wasn't built from struggle or complexity—
for she has never existed,

and never will.

- The Reason -

I wept the most out of everyone in my home.
Spilt milk on the table
would release the floodgates—
tears rushing from my eyes.

Now, I'm not the victim—
some pathetic girl who cries
at the dinner table
every second night.

I thought I'd love to be the one
in control of my emotions,
but it hurts more
to cause someone else's
timorous explosions.

- The Reason -

I've been called an enabler
once or twice.

When kindness feels unnatural
and neglect
is the factory setting,
nothing hurts as badly
as begging
for a mother's love.

So I do it,
and I'll do it again.

Fear of disappointment
is greater than any spider,
any height,
any depth.

Her embrace strangles me,
but her abandonment
feels much, much worse.

- The Reason -

I can only act on what I know—
swinging doors and swinging moods.

My eyes leaked themselves dry
the first week of my life.
Now I'm inured to the chaos
of turbulent changes in the wind
that cause doors to slam shut
and rashes to form on skin.

- The Reason -

As a child,
I slept on the floor
to act as a door weight
when the lock and chain
couldn't hold back
the man *she* had betrayed.

That's when my body
became a shield—
one that no longer
belonged to me.

- The Reason -

Why am I still crying
over a lack of love
from the woman who birthed me?

It's been a decade
since she left this earth—
and even longer since
she slammed the door in my face,

when I tried putting out the fires
ignited in her heart
by arsonist-lovers
she knew were only set on
destroying her—

acrimony is hereditary.

- The Reason -

I know object permanence
develops in infancy,
but I'm accustomed to abandonment
and struggle to believe
I'll still exist to you
if I'm further than your eyes can see.

*I'm scared you'll forget and leave me,
just like everyone else leaves me.*

- The Reason -

I've told you time and time again:
I can't control the weather.

- The Reason -

My blood feels thick,
as though I can feel it
forcing its way through each branched vein
in order to keep me alive.

It's a painful effort
to stretch what remains
after being so torturously drained—
as it coagulates to keep
the centre of my chest beating.

I fear the only way to thin my blood
enough to reach my extremities
will be the cause of my demise.

As it was with my mother.

- The Reason -

God fucked my girlfriend
when I was fifteen
and asked me to excuse
his behaviour.

Forgiveness came easy—
just not to me,
in that town.

She said she was bored,
so I forgave her
and accepted eternity in hell
for a dalliance
with a saint.

She was my saviour.
Where was hers?

- The Reason -

My table seats six,
but only one chair bears weight.

Ghosts of the people I loved
sit for a meal—
but they don't eat,
so I don't either.

The absence of people to care for
asserts my grief is never-ending.

- The Reason -

I am the way you yell,
the way you worry.

I am tall,
lanky,
and I can be funny—
but I am sick.
Sicker than you.

Thoughts so harsh
ascertained
why we're such pricks,
and I'm sorry.

- The Reason -

I can only love fully—

It's a tiresome fault
for a girl to give all she is
before a deal is made.

- The Reason -

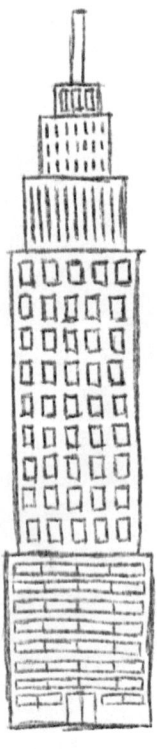

My lens reflects the world
far removed from yours.
Because there is no ground
in front of your feet,
you take a step forward
without falling to your rest.

When I go to follow
but the drop is too steep,
I'll take a step backwards—

because I believe what *I* see.

- The Reason -

The tiny, violent creature
with innate belligerence
is combative by precaution,
as though the world
will only ever do her wrong.

No one asks why a wasp stings—
they just do.

- The Reason -

I inhaled smoke from the doused wick before I knew,
as though I was warned in genesis
how hard it was going to get.

I breathed in before
the air around me thickened;
now my lungs feel lighter
than they should.

Premonition.

- The Reason -

I'm a pomegranate peeler—

someone who would peel one for a stranger,
spending hours, days, years
taking apart the membranes,
loving and nurturing flesh
for each tiny, painstaking seed.

But I'm getting tired.

I can't stop peeling pomegranates
for people
who don't even fucking like them.

- The Reason -

I'll eat my weight in stress,
rile her up before I leave,
so you can see
what a mess she is
compared to what she used to be.

- The Reason -

You no longer have to worry
about that hideous smile
escaping from the corners of your lips;
you're safe now, darling,
from hiding your admiration
for anything.

- The Reason -

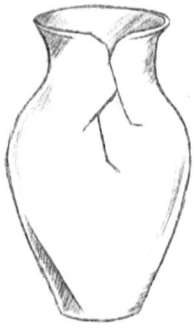

An unconvincing fake—
my exterior was made of mouldable clay,
ready to be manipulated
by whoever deemed me worthy to touch.

Never fired long enough to keep my shape,
and too many cracks to be worth purchasing—
for the likelihood of shattering within their hands
is almost certain.

A fragile personality.

- The Reason -

I suffix meaning to conjunctions,
stripped from incoherent conversations,
background noise,
and nothing.

This subterfuge of first-person writing
is not derived from experiences
I have been directly involved in—
rather, ones of other versions of myself
living perpetually in my head,
with an enhanced dialect
and confidence
I don't harness in the flesh.

- The Reason -

Inconvenient
Misanthropic

Selfish
Obsessive
Resentful
Reckless
Yours

How painful it must be to be loved by me.

- The Reason -

A guaranteed outcome,
but never in my favour.

All in on red.

I'll bet on misfortune—
it's the only thing I'm sure of.

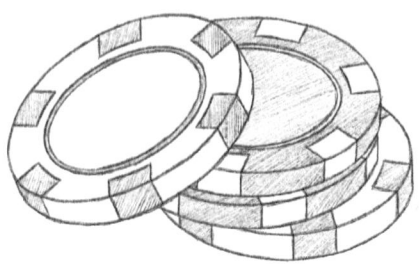

- The Reason -

How can one leaf
fear so strongly
falling wrongly,
while simultaneously
fearing falling perfectly
in line?

*I've always been good
at taking on bad advice.*

- The Reason -

When your guardian angel
wears the face of your deepest regret,
her guidance wanes.

Worship the villain.

Hard to believe redemption
was hiding in such a ruinous state.

Your world's upside down, girl—
shake his hand,
or you'll be on your own.

- The Reason -

I lost my mind when we lost you.

I saw you driving to see us,
but I hadn't told you
we had already left.

Such innocence and effort—
to drive all that way
just to turn back.

The next time we came to see you,
you had left.

Now guilt erodes my mind,
and I no longer feel
as welcomed as I once was
in a family—
because you loved us more than anything.

- The Reason -

I understand the affinity
for exploring ruins;
after all,
a shipwreck
is still a sight to behold.

I'm just more fragile than before.

The Cause

- The Cause -

It might have hit different
if it was the first time
I'd heard it.

*This is what happens
to little bitch girls
that don't listen—*

you sound just like my dad.

- The Cause -

His slender fingers know
the passcode to my life.

Too dumb to capitulate
to his needs.
Don't be stubborn, you.
Be his.

- The Cause -

He trained me—
just as his father trained his mother.

He abandoned me outside,
kicked me through the cut-out of the door
and told me to stay.

Of course I did.
I loved him.

I just hoped he'd come back soon.

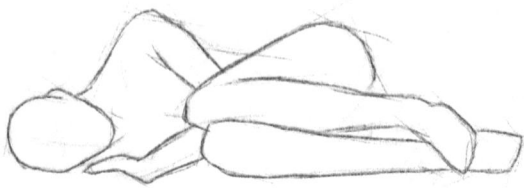

- The Cause -

The first time he raised his fist,
I didn't flinch.

I wasn't scared
because I didn't know
what was coming.

He loved me that morning.

The second time, I deserved it.

'You said you loved me unconditionally.'
So I served him while bleeding.

And I bled every time after that.

- The Cause -

I'll never understand trauma
and its power to make you need what you hate.

How what hurts you
becomes your faith.

- The Cause -

Every man I've prayed to
is marred by flaws,
like the inaccuracies in the Bible
the pious choose to ignore.

- The Cause -

Discovers solace in amber brew.
You leave love at home
and rally friendship with flies—
but the flies return home to their families
and leave you wasted,

but not before they lay eggs
and overrun your every waking thought.

The eggs hatch into maggots,
replacing those already rotting in your brain
from the week before,

only to be replaced again—

Friday.

Saturday.

Sunday.

Tuesday?

Why on a fucking Tuesday?

Who knew a maggot could control a man?

Eventually, you're convinced
to swallow enough Dutch courage
to ruin a life.

And you do.
Ruin a life.

Ruin *my* life.

- The Cause -

It's feeling outnumbered
in a room with one other person.

All you have to do
is be in the wrong place
at the wrong time,
and look damn good.

Irresistible.

- The Cause -

I'm a statistic—

the ones they teach in high school
about consent,

the ones mothers
warn their daughters about
walking home at night.

One that I promised
I would never let myself become.

Too strong to let a man
take control of me—
until I wasn't.

I couldn't stop him,
so I let him.

And then I married him.
And became another statistic.

- The Cause -

He would rape his wife
as she cried,
stone cold sober.

Still, I gifted him a life.

I don't deserve to be her mother.

My greatest achievement
and my biggest regret.

Mummy loves you xx

- The Cause -

The monster,
he jumped the counter—

but he didn't want what was in the register;
he wanted me—

the cashier.

- The Cause -

I wish I'd admitted sooner
that I knew he wore a different skin.

I should have knelt in penance
to atone for all his sins—

but the devil pays no heed
to his wrongdoings
to repent.

My only prayer—
despite her father—

is that she is heaven sent.

- The Cause -

The biggest words come out of a man's mouth
when his ego hurts—
as though his vocabulary only expands
with collapse.

It's just a shame
he couldn't use his words
to prevent this in the first place.

- The Cause -

He said he'd rather fuck a corpse—
maybe then he'd feel more.

I wish he'd just cut off my head
instead of killing me
from the inside out.

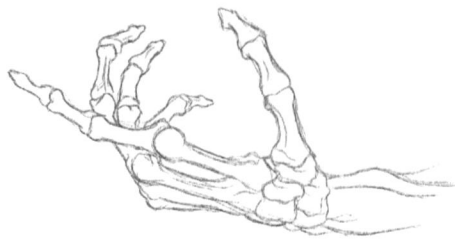

- The Cause -

I need a manly man,
but in a softer way.

Maybe she will treat my body the way it deserves.
I don't need to tell her it's not okay;
she knows—
and wouldn't dream of trying.

No longer fighting,
I've forgotten how to say no—
because she just knows.

- The Cause -

Knowing you have the power to hurt me
must feel like such a rush,
so I understand the buzz
when you slip,
and I run right back
with my hands and heart open again.

I know my weakness
only tempts your tastebuds
when it's a result of your destruction.

Build me up,
so you can tear me down.

- The Cause -

The day I realised
the only good you had
was good that I created—

you became irreversibly insufferable.

- The Cause -

Solace ignores me
like I'm a charity fundraiser
at a shopfront's entrance.

The Cause

Hands around my throat,
I was dragged over the threshold,
so I packed its bags
and sent my home away.

I would rather burn alive
than step inside again.

- The Cause -

A fervent desire
to get inside your mind,
fuck your brain,
then push out your eyes—
let them dangle down your cheeks.

I'll knock out all your teeth,
pull your tongue
back into your throat,
then jump out your nose
to watch you choke—

oh, what a sight.

- The Cause -

The satisfaction
of watching the devil
burn himself to bones
is greater
than any revenge.

- The Cause -

You make me feel
there's nothing I can't afford
in a world I rule—
a realm of misbehaviour,

because I'm in Hell's hell—

and I pay to control it,
to stop it from emulating life on Earth
with you.

- The Cause -

You must have realised
I was an actress
long before I gave up my career.

It's tiresome
working for a man
who can't pay you—
or make you come.

- The Cause -

It's volition we lack.
We make decisions
based on what men want.

We've been conditioned
to think it's safer—

ignore our guts
and listen to theirs.

She was inflicted with pain
she didn't let in.
If the mat doesn't say *'welcome,'*
don't cum in.

- The Cause -

Something to make my splitting mind
more black and white—

now I see evil,
and only evil,
in what I once loved.

- The Cause -

She's not in tune with my emotions
the way she thinks she is.

If she was, she'd know
I've never been more afraid
of letting myself go.

To her, it's just another Tuesday—
and I'm happy for her, I suppose.

- The Cause -

I've confused chemistry with compatibility—
thought they were one and the same.

Why would you give yourself so freely
just to take it away?

If you think you can have me back,
don't.

- The Cause -

I didn't agree to an entente.
You promised to fight.

This covenant can't survive
if your only strategy
is to keep yourself alive.

- The Cause -

It's exhausting
being under your spotlight all the time—
my actions decrypted
and repeated back to me.

You call it love,
I call it being overanalysed.

- The Cause -

I stretch myself too thin—
too quick to fold into your absence,
too eager to fill the quiet.

We are anxious attachment.

- The Cause -

I can't tell if your abandonment
is an attempt to *save* me
from your collapse,
or if you've simply forgotten
masochist is my middle name.

- The Cause -

'Do you have thoughts of hurting yourself
or others?'
I can't even count
how many times
I've been asked.

I wish it was others—

but I'm no killer.

The Cause

She developed a dichotomous mind.
Baptism by fire.

It split her right down the middle—
a division
of black and white.

And she came out,
only half alive.

- The Cause -

It's ironic—
the one who made me want to fall in love again,
and the one who made me wish I could forget how,

are both the same person.

- The Cause -

I was already alone.
Now I just sleep alone, too.

You can find me in your dreams.

- The Cause -

Writing that appeals to you
because you're me in another life—
brimming with emotions,
no appetite,
and a mouth of decay.

To elicit those feelings for you,
from me, and reciprocate
your ignorance to my suffering…

You'll never know how I sound to me,
and I'll never want you again.

- The Cause -

It's like finding your way back—
after half your life in constant storms—
to a locked door with no key.

You've found a window that needs fixing,
and perhaps that's your way in—
except she cuts you on entry
and leaves an ugly reminder
of how close you almost were
to being home.

- The Cause -

Masqueraded as an invitation,
motivated ill intention,
and nullified my consent
for a stranger to pursue me.

It's no wonder I disparage
my femininity—

she betrayed me.

- The Cause -

The passion radiating from her chest
is dampened
by an anxious mind
begging to be freed,
pleading to be seen.

I wonder how she'd feel
if she let go—
let her heart take control.

I guess she's afraid
of paying mind
to everything she's worked so hard to hide.

- The Cause -

He lived like that because he knew
he could break into heaven
and make everyone believe
that's where he was supposed to be.

- The Cause -

The conversation beforehand
threw me off my game.
I wonder if talking to you
is what cursed my day.

Post hoc ergo propter hoc.

- The Cause -

I lull myself
with the comfort of repetition—
safety in knowing what comes next.

The absence of something, anything,
has me gripping at my chest.

Tell me how you so easily put this to bed,
so I might stop the unrest
usurping my head.

- The Cause -

Entered my email address voluntarily:
a subscription to heartbreak.

I signed up for this?

UNSUBSCRIBE
UNSUBSCRIBE
UNSUBSCRIBE

- The Cause -

An unforgiving vision—
she was the only other person
who could see it.

A concentric target.
Insentient man.
A filthy mess.

She cried
and cried
and cried
and cried.

- The Cause -

When even the neighbourhood narcissist
said this was going to end badly,
running was the right idea—
but not back to you.

It's just a force of habit.

I'm not ready to learn my lesson.

- The Cause -

The decision was made—
no goodbyes.

One last petty attempt
at holding you accountable.

Perhaps a manslaughter charge
as a parting gift.

You owe her a life—
and not just because I love her.

She convinced me
I don't want to rid myself of the world anymore—
even if only
not to do you a favour.

But she'll avenge me
if I do.

The Longing

- The Longing -

I'm not hapless when it comes to love.
Rather,
I'm hapless with the feelings
associated with love.

- The Longing -

Loving you is difficult—

despite being so easy to love,
I've never met so much resistance
to finding something good.

- The Longing -

I'd call it beginners luck,
except I think you know what you're doing.

Spectators whisper over my shoulder.
They've been watching your next move for
weeks— and I hear them sigh
when I let you take me.

I'm trapped
exactly where I want to be—
between the knight and the queen.

Checkmate.

I didn't want to win anyway.

- The Longing -

It was a forfeit
long before we noticed.

I heard one say,
'She wrought oblation of her Queen!'

Because hearts
are not pawns, my love.

Stalemate is all we'll ever be.

- The Longing -

'Be unwilling to lie to yourself'
was the guidance given
from the little pill with the fortune
inside

So tell me why,
once I convince myself
I deserve more than you offer,
I feel I've committed perjury—
and either way, I've lied.

If they still executed,
I'd be dead.

- The Longing -

It would be the worst thing of all
to find out
you don't think of me.

Even with my eyes closed,
I find something of you
in everything.

- The Longing -

I pray my unyielding offers of affection
aren't dimmed by their abundance—
on the contrary,
I mean them more each time.

- The Longing -

The romantic in me
has no autonomy.

I don't get to decide
how much of me is given.

- The Longing -

It wasn't meant to be anything else.
It wasn't meant to *mean* anything else.

But it did,
and it does,
and I can't take it back
without some kind of lobotomy.

Please,

cut open my brain,
take out the parts
that can't function
without you—
because it wasn't meant to be like this.

- The Longing -

I want to squeeze you dry
until there's nothing left to guess,
then gently put you aside
like every lover I've ever left.

- The Longing -

Where can I put it
so it won't find its way?

I tried locking it up.
I drove for hours,
meaning to leave it
somewhere far away.

I even embraced it,
hoping it would get sick of me
and leave on its own.

But it came back—
took rest in my head
with all intention to stay.

She lives here clandestinely.

- The Longing -

Like the details of a dream
upon waking.
Like my confidence
when talking to someone attractive.
Like my competence at work
when the boss is around.

Let it defy me,
escape me,
evade me.

Let it elude me.

- The Longing -

So absorbed in myself,
I'll take every opportunity
to get you back
to the place
where I take priority
over your compunction.

A confession.

- The Longing -

I don't want to fall in love,
so I will walk this place
with my head down and my eyes closed—
averting the gaze
of potential lovers.

- The Longing -

I tell myself each morning:
the love I give
is not equal to
the love I receive—

because no one
is as extraordinary as me.

Surely I'm not
as unlovable as I feel.

- The Longing -

Slaloming through your moods
and formidable intelligence—
the kind of intellect
that makes having a conversation with you
feel like an accomplishment.

- The Longing -

Her utterances bemuse me.
Contradictions,
one line
to the next.

I'm desperate to believe her,
to save what's in my chest.

Instead, I'll count on daisies
to put my heart at rest—

She loves me…
she loves me not…
she loves me…

she loves—

- The Longing -

He only wants me
when he's thinking of her.

As though you can only have one true love—
and everyone else
is just a reminder
of what once was.

- The Longing -

It's instinctual
and physically impossible to withhold—
a most natural reaction.

Like a moth to a flame,
I'd give anything to have it—
and give anything to take the need away.

- The Longing -

Sugar and gelatine,
his words stick to my teeth
like candy—
eloquence wrapped in sweetness.

He takes my side
every time.

But my mouth is full of cavities
that need filling
before I can consume
any more saccharine verbiage
from him.

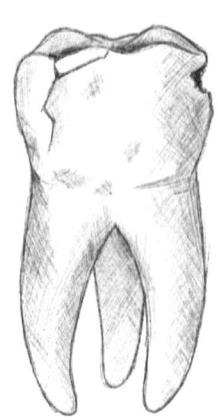

- The Longing -

I filled every second of my time with her—
I thought it made me valuable.

I'm not what she needs
in her time of need,
like she is for me.

Now, I'm alone again.

- The Longing -

I would damage us
in those times of need.
Don't be fooled
into thinking it's copacetic.
Solitary is not a preference—
rather, my only choice
in upholding us.

I need to be alone again.
I'm sorry.

- The Longing -

Nothing like
fucking up
my only chance
to exist in your world.

- The Longing -

I wonder if *he* feels the same as I do.
If he's willing to put his life on the line,
just as I would for you.

At what point does discomfort
trump your happiness?
Where is the line
where self-preservation takes priority
and his emotions outweigh yours?

No such line exists in me.

The Longing

The second-hand guilt
should be too much to bear.

My selfishness for you
aligns perfectly
with my moral culpability.

My narcissism begs for your adoration—
no matter the cost.

I know you don't have money to spare.

- The Longing -

The pixelated version of you
is much more innocent.
The distorted audio
enhances your placation.

It *sounds* like you care.

The screen casts light
to the dark spots under your eyes,
and you almost smile.

That's all you have to do.

Find somewhere to rest your eyes,
and blink
when deemed appropriate.

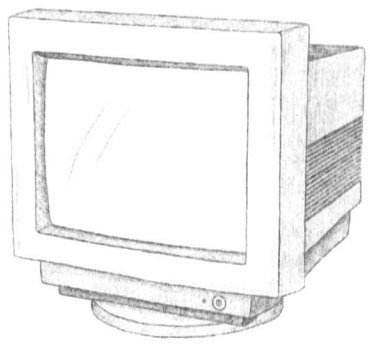

- The Longing -

You know,
if it melts into carnal heat
and burns away the threshold
of platonic distance between,

I'd make a break for it—
faster than regret could catch up.

So you can play this game too.

Go hard, baby,
because there's nothing to lose
when there's nothing to win.

And there's nothing to win.

- The Longing -

Our existence is only temporary.
So I'll be reckless with my heart.

I'd rather risk it all and fail
than be scared of love
and fail anyway.

Be reckless with me.

- The Longing -

Abate my struggle
by being here.
Share with me your kind eyes.
Curtail my life
with your existence.

Alas—
those who love
are those who die.

- The Longing -

I'll feign being cold
to eclipse my nerves.

What folly—
to convulse like this
for someone I am not with,
under a sky I don't belong beneath.

- The Longing -

She is Valium,
and I pray for an unlimited supply:
-without prescription.
-willingly over-sedated.

I forget I'm predisposed to addiction.

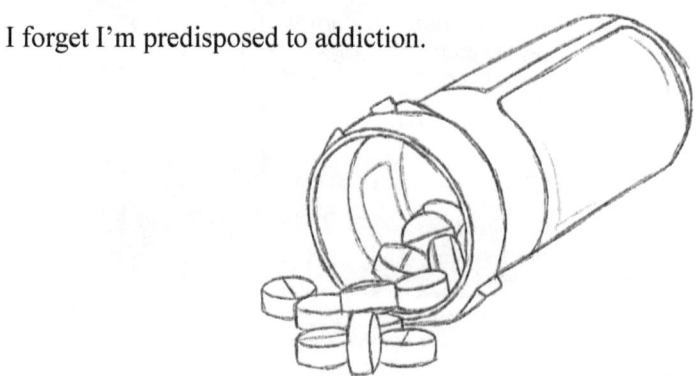

- The Longing -

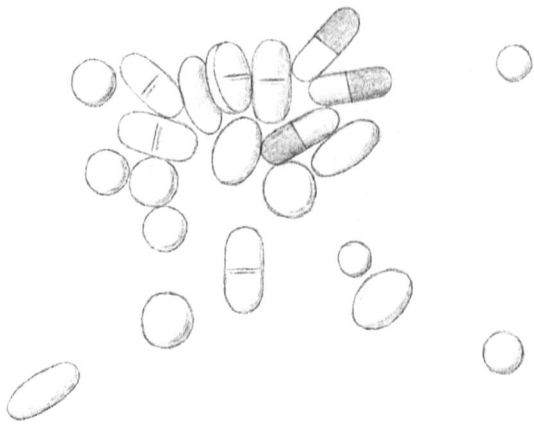

- The Longing -

Don't expect me to play the role
of your protagonist
when love doesn't transpire for me
as the director of a scene
where the one that I love
abandons me.

Cut.

- The Longing -

My script was worded differently
than the rest of the cast's—
an alternate ending
everyone looked past.

I felt the sideline characters
needn't waste their time;

when the heroine loves her back,
it ends perfectly in mine.

- The Longing -

I fear the arrhythmia
will expose me
if it hasn't already.

The desperation is revolting.
This is revolting.
But I'm addicted to the high.

Left alone to withdraw,
she loads another hit.

I thought she wanted me sober?

- The Longing -

I already knew
when the idea of someone else
felt like a betrayal—

not to you,
but to me.

- The Longing -

Why is it called *stealing* a heart
when the thief merely exists,
and the victim scripts the tale
by giving it away
so willingly?

- The Longing -

Left unattended,
my heart wasn't stolen—
it was an innocent casualty.

She's no thief.
Just an opportunist.
…maybe.

- The Longing -

Hold my wearied body
the way you hold space
for my thoughts
and my downfalls—
effortlessly,
without temptation.

Hold me until sleep drags me under.

The sweetest of dreams.

- The Longing -

I've begged the world
to stop this pretence.
It bugs me,
you know,
how others are enthralled by you,
and all you are
is rude,
but sure,
surer than the fall of night
ensuing sleep—

sure.
I'll be yours.

Just not yours to keep.

- The Longing -

Of course my gaze found her.
It always does—
a burning stare
locks to mine
as I realise
I've bookmarked each freckle
on her cheek
more times than I care to count.

And I'm caught again—

my retinas burnt
with repetitive daydreams—

I could draw her, you know.

- The Longing -

How do I explicate
she is every colour
of a sunset in January?

- The Longing -

I need her in the night especially—
a distraction from what plagues me.

As darkness closes in,
she is Soteria—

goddess, you are salvation.

- The Longing -

To say you are everything
I've ever dreamed of
would be untruthful.

I just hope
to never dream of anything else.

- The Longing -

Ensconce me in your presence,
touch me with your whispers,
let me claim your smile—
it's mine now.

I refuse to stir from sleep,
not wanting to re-enter a world
where I'm a stranger
to what I need.

- The Longing -

The morning after you,
I realised,
I'd never been angry with the sun
for rising.

- The Longing -

Take your time.
There's no rush.

I see it's superficial.
The closet isn't made of glass—
baby, it's made of crystal.

I see right through you.

- The Longing -

I can give you the world,
take you where you've only dreamed.
Between your crisp white sheets,
I'll lay out my promises
while you lay in my arms.

This is what I mean.
Let me show you what could be.

I'll love you infinitely—
if you'll let me.

- The Longing -

You make me a wallflower in my own dreams.
I watch you tumble through my mind
from quiet corners, hoping you'll see.

Defy unrequited love.
You smile *through* me.
After all,
I am asleep.

Do we kiss in your dreams too?

- The Longing -

Your alacrity to help me survive here
will put me in your bed,

making it impossible to endure,
withstand,
or overcome
the absence of you.

- The Longing -

I know your love would ruin me—
and I would let it.
I'd invite it in,
make it coffee,
sleep in past twelve
just to be closer longer.

I wish I could live
without wondering
how far I want to cross the line.
We're just friends—
and that has to be fine.

- The Longing -

Let's sit on opposite sides of the room.
I don't want your arm brushing up against mine.

I'd rather play tug of war
with your eyes,
from afar.

Pull me in,
tug me back and forth.
Neither of us willing to give.

Tension tightens—
but nobody wins.

- The Longing -

No time has ever been,
or will ever be,
enough
to explore the contours of her body,
mapping the geography of her pleasure.

I know her better
than the back of my own hand—
the same hands
that brought her to my bed
and keep her there.

Her movements are precise, delicate—
as if reading my mind,
acting before I think
my thoughts into existence.

She takes my breath away.
Every. Single. Time.

I fear I'll never feel sated.

- The Longing -

My body reacts without control.
So ashamedly possessive.

I want to protect her so badly,
rationality is no longer something I know
or believe in.

- The Longing -

She tempts my faith—
with no backbone,
it reflexively abdicates
for any attention
thrown my way.

- The Longing -

I trail my fingers along my body,
envisioning the possibility of you.

Unseen yet felt—
you flourish in places
you've never existed.

- The Longing -

Only those you've allowed
to share your lips
could know what fire tastes like.

Please, let me burn.

- The Longing -

If this lifetime isn't ours,
take me to the next.
Because I only learned
life is too short
after knowing you
in this one.

- The Longing -

Take what's yours.
Slip through the cracks of self-control.
Help me let go.

Give in to temptation.
The guards have gone home—
invade me.

- The Longing -

If her smile makes you feel that much,
just think what she's capable of
with her touch.

- The Longing -

She is KING.

She doesn't know the power she holds.
Through a stranger's eyes,
she is bold.

Through mine—
she is unearthly.

- The Longing -

I hope you know—
all the things you ever asked of me
and I refused,
I do for her
with pleasure.

- The Longing -

Every time he touched me,
I pictured her instead.

He felt so big and manly,
but she was in my head.

- The Longing -

She's convinced she can conceal it,
camouflage her heart.
But I see the way her pupils dilate.

She can silence her thoughts—
but her body speaks my language.

- The Longing -

I've undressed her with every glance.
My mind drifts to darker places,
where my thoughts unravel
at the thought of unravelling her.

Pulling at the edges of reason,
I have no boundaries.

Oh gods.
Not here.
Not now.

- The Longing -

I want you so bad.
Baby,
I watch your apparition
in my bedroom.

When I undress,
we lock eyes—
and I welcome
that insidious grin.

- The Longing -

The inflection of your voice
    ebbs
           and
                  flows
                          with intensity.

When fervour infuses the words you speak,
it ecstasises me.
But what gets me even more,
I ruefully confess,
is how your patience quivers
when you speak of loathing, hatred, and contempt.

Reveal the vastness of your aversions,
disdains, and regrets.
Capturing the echoes of your flaws,
I'm nothing short of obsessed.

How can feelings of such displeasure
elicit these musings of sex?

Your anathemas pronounce
my devotion to you *(the real you)*.

- The Longing -

Of all the lines I've overstepped,
you're the hardest secret
I've never kept.

- The Longing -

Let's start the morning with a fight,
so we can make subsequent love.
I promise,
I will be better than I was.

The Longing

I'll come back for you.

On the day my attention is sparse
and my social limits are met,
I'll come back for you.

On the day the blue all but consumes me,
and I fear I mightn't recover,
I'll come back for you.

On the day another lover leaves
the comfort of my bed,
I'll come back for you.

On the day of your epiphany,
when *meant to be* is reality,
come back to me.

And when that time comes—
and it will—
I'll come back for you.

The Longing

I wish I could
bottle the electricity
pulsing through me
when you're happy.
When you laugh.

When you…
When you…
When you…

Bottled adrenaline electrifies me.
When you—

- The Longing -

I won't give voice to what sits heavy.
Don't worry—
connected by tension,
I sense your thoughts
just as you sense mine.
It's fine, I know.

Telepathist.

- The Longing -

We live in a world that belongs to you.

I wish you existed in mine,
where you are unnerved,
and I am
impossible to you.

Stand by...

- The Longing -

Give me a reason to hate you,
because I hate wanting you,
and I love not needing you.

I need you to hate not wanting me.

- The Longing -

She could take me apart,
piece by piece,
and I would be grateful.

The distance between us
is slim.

I love her enough to let her
destroy me—
and I know she will.

- The Longing -

Consumed by desire
for something
I don't even want.

My mind is blank with stupidity,
writing a soap opera of my life.

Melodramatic reactions
match my efficiency
in feeling more noticed than I am.

Static shots of vacuous sentiments
broken by your recoil and unease.
Because extended intervals mean nothing to you
when our eyes meet.

- The Longing -

She circumvents my attempts
to keep my mind free of her,
bypasses security,
then smiles at me
on her way to my hippocampus.

My servers have been infiltrated.

- The Longing -

How can I emote solicitude
without provoking your salvo?
Because I've forgotten my vest,
and my only chance to get close
is to expose my assailable chest.

I'm at your mercy now.

- The Longing -

I've never so strongly felt something
intangible.
I know it's just a theory—
the force of something material is
easily explained,
but how do I elucidate
that I am so tightly bound to you
it feels like chains?

String is too fragile,
too delicate
to hold me like this.

- The Longing -

You were my cachet,
proof that I was worth wanting—
and I was a luxury brand
maintained to perfection.

But when they stole the badge
from the bonnet,
I crashed the car into a tree,
poured gasoline on it,
and fled the scene.

- The Longing -

She isn't just pretty,
adorned by beauty—
she's every definition of the word.

Enamoured by her spirit,
I'm frozen in time,
like an absent seizure,
and I'm elated to stay.

- The Longing -

I remembered all the digits to your number—
never saved them in my phone—
ten characters in an arbitrary sequence,
along with the address of your home.

One day,
I'll call you drunk
from memory,
just to ask if you're still alone.

If you change your number,
or I forget the placement of a figure,
I'll reach a stranger's dial tone.

- The Longing -

Inspiration does exist,
but it must find you working.

To watch
you be you
is a most beautiful thing.

- The Longing -

I commandeered your iridescent eyes
to look my way,
because I drown in the seriousness
of what you do to my thoughts
when you abstain from neglecting
our gut-aching,
pride-breaking,
deficient existence
in each other's lives.

- The Longing -

There's an unfinished conversation,
disturbed by an apology of sorts.

Elongated silence
promises me
a place in the line of people
you will see,
because, if the conversation never happens,
I will always be
first in line,
out the front,
blithely waiting to go in.

- The Longing -

I call you by a name
no one else calls you,
and we don't tell anyone
because they don't want to know—
our interest in ourselves,
or our interest
in each other's interest in ourselves.

- The Longing -

My favourite colour
used to be pink,
but I've indulged in you
too long—
you're now all I remember.

Everything you are
metamorphosed into me;
I am no longer myself,

but I'm definitely better.

- The Longing -

Dog-ear my pages—
crease me
so I remember you were here.

- The Longing -

My goal was to give off different impressions
to everyone,
but I got too good at pretending
each of them was you.

- The Longing -

It's just like you
to recite a platitude like
'take the good with the bad.'

I'll take suffering.
I'll take weakness.
I'll take blame.

I'll take all of it
in exchange
for the parts of yourself
you don't offer
to anyone else.

- The Longing -

I'm yet to find a piece of you
that doesn't entirely overwhelm me
in all of the best ways.

I'm not afraid of you.

You are welcomed here.
All of you,
in all your forms.

I can love each one separately—
and together,
all at once,
whole—with me.

- The Longing -

- The Longing -

She surrenders to the stillness,
takes refuge
beneath the surface tension—
her head underwater
to keep her mind quiet.

I'm never sure
if she thinks I'm trying to drown her,
or if she knows how badly
I want to keep her alive,
despite the barotrauma of trying.

The depths don't have what you're looking for.

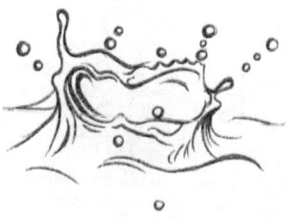

- The Longing -

Her impatience with me is certain
from deep under the surface.

She finds a broken brain funny—
she laughs a lot.
I hurt her too often
for her to not want
to drown me
and finally finish the job.

But I'll hold her head under, too,
until the splashing stops.

Is this where we'll spend eternity?

- The Longing -

'Operator—what's your emergency?'

'She's holding my heart for ransom and is threatening to kill me.'

'Ma'am, the culprit has no weapons; have you tried walking away?'

- The Longing -

If you get me on my own
and there is
something on your mind,

know that I want to know—

even if it shakes
our comfortable nothing.

- The Longing -

She's not afraid of heights,
but I know she's scared
of falling.

- The Longing -

If you could point out
all the parts of you
you don't love,
I'll start from there
and work my way up.

- The Longing -

She wrote a soft poem,
and started a war in my mind.
I heard her cadence
lilting through the lyrics,
reminding me of what I have
and how I feel about it.

I'll make her cry
at least ten more times
before she packs up her heart,
takes off
without goodbye,
and rewraps it
as a gift
for someone
more fitting than me.

The Cure

- The Cure -

Green-eyed and soft-spoken,
she shifts atmospheres with her presence,
inspires just by being.

I know love exists
because she's here.

If I could repeat life again,
I would make every step the same,
knowing our paths will cross when they do.

Like a ghost, she moves
through the walls I've built
and, without words,
heals wounds she didn't cause.

What if this time it's not too good to be true?
What if something so admirable
could enter my life and stay?

Surely I couldn't be so fortuitous.

- The Cure -

Hitherto,
I was living in a world that forgot my name,
or used it only to exploit my pain.

Unheld by meaning,
consumed by blue,
this life was cruel—
but then came you.

- The Cure -

It's like we've met before—
perhaps in another time,
as children, or
maybe even lovers.

Engraved into my soul,
I'm not me without you.

You are worth the wait,
in this lifetime
and the next.

Once my eyelids touch,
I begin to dream.

Wait for me—
I'll meet you there.

- The Cure -

Maybe I knew all along
that we were going to meet.

I studied my words vigorously,
committed their meanings to memory,
so I could form strings
and curate these lines to define
what you mean to me.

- The Cure -

I'd make her suffering
my last meal
if it would die with me.

- The Cure -

It's as though we reinvented love
to fill the gaps we were missing—

You make me whole again.

- The Cure -

I'll never forget your calls.
When I couldn't breathe,
or talk,
or see.

In the depths of misery,
your voice
was just for me.

Don't hang up.

- The Cure -

There's a lot I'm unsure of,
but I've realised,
life is infinitely more beautiful
since you've arrived…

And it's not just because I love flowers.

- The Cure -

Little me
dreamed of you,
but it's better late
than never.

'How long have you two been friends?'

- The Cure -

Little me
can't believe
she wins the lottery.

Let's make up for lost time.

- The Cure -

When I met you,
I felt like I'd finally met myself.

If someone as extraordinary as you
can find the good in me,
maybe there is something worthwhile
here after all.

- The Cure -

My stars fit with yours
to create constellations.

Everyone around us sees them too.

I feel their admiration for what we are
and their awe
at how you put light in my eyes.

- The Cure -

I give love freely—
it flows out of me in excess.

I give myself permission—
without rules
or restrictions—
to believe
this is where
and how
I'm meant to be.

I trust in serendipity.

- The Cure -

- The Cure -

I won't tattoo my skin.
Not because it hurts,
but because I've never kept anything
long-term.

Our flame will only continue to burn
if we stay out of each other's beds—

we are more than want,
more than fire fed by flesh.

We are what stays when heat fades—

love me the way I want you to love me.

- The Cure -

Perhaps you've never held on to anything long-term
because no one has ever shown up
the way you deserve.

Still,
I'll love you the way *you* want me to,
and it will have to be enough—
because we don't get to mess this one up.

This flame won't die…
without a revolution.

Game rules:

1. If I win, she loses.
2. If she loses, I also lose.
3. If she wins, I'm not a part of the game.

Any way we play, I've lost.

- The Cure -

I should make it clear:
I don't want this game to end.

I'll face the final boss
with open arms,
and if she cuts off my head,
I'll respawn in front of her
and face her down again.

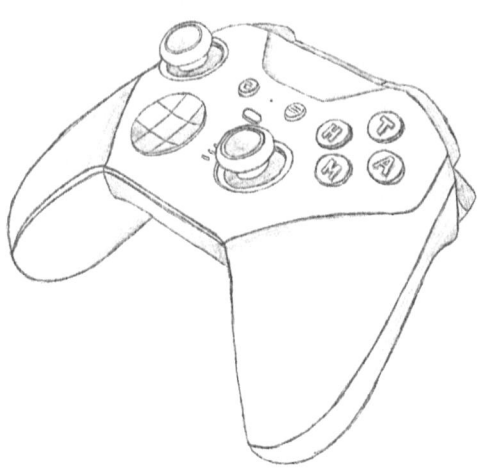

The final boss
wasn't put at the end of the game
to destroy you—
but to crown you
with a victory.

- The Cure -

There's no need for patience
in this house-fire of a relationship—

we're going to end it
before you can claim insurance.

I'll toss the keys into the blaze
and dare you to stay inside.

You'll come out with burns,
scorched and bitter,
but not surprised.

We get on like a house on fire!

- The Cure -

I feel time and distance
like tangible objects—
bands at constant stretch,
bringing me back
to a place and time
where we were together.

How am I supposed to be
without her?

I don't think I am.

- The Cure -

Two solipsists can't exist
at the same time,
yet somehow,
I'm inside your mind,
and you're inside mine.

One can't subsist without the other.

That's what they call a soul-tie.

- The Cure -

Even if we had it all together,
I'd probably still run late,
and you would still spill your coffee.

But we would have it all…

Together.

- The Cure -

It feels good
imitating the parts of you
I love.

Pretending I'm you,
just to feel loved
by me.

- The Cure -

- The Cure -

I don't deserve her
or what she stands for.
Being loved and wanted
clashes with my history.

I know she likes the taste
of being seen, but
my despondency
trumps her love.

She doesn't understand
how it helps her miss me.

Still, I miss her more.

- The Cure -

She is worthy of more
than I have to offer.

Still, I offer all I am
in a desperate attempt
to break through
her dejection.

My disposition to please her
is met with privation,
so I simply crave her—

to crave me more.

- The Cure -

I won't demarcate your heart—
because you need
the electricity
of two free things.

We'll pull each other
from the dark—
this is laissez-faire.

That's the deal—
no deal at all,
just the thrill of staying
without being held.

- The Cure -

She tells me:

*The day after a night with you
feels lonelier
than the day after a divorce.*

- The Cure -

Her heart races
at the slightest hint of rejection.

Not rejection from people—
there are too many fish in the sea—
but rejection from the goals
she so badly wants to achieve.

- The Cure -

I now realise
my highest standards
were always low-hanging fruit—
the bare-minimum type.

She woke me up
before I even realised
what she was doing.

I don't think she meant it.
I don't dream alone anymore.

My love is valuable—
I am deserving of something better
than I've ever received before.

- The Cure -

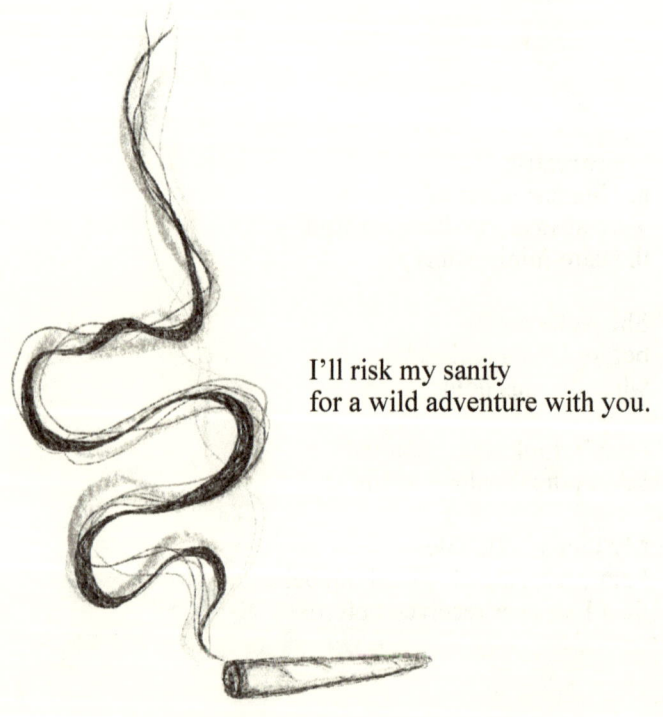

I'll risk my sanity
for a wild adventure with you.

- The Cure -

For as long as I exist,
someone will love
every version of you—
willingly.

- The Cure -

She's better than I am
in every way—
vivifies the world with her art,
makes others feel safe,
asking for nothing in return
except the exemption of abuse,
because that is all she has ever been—
the subject of misuse.

- The Cure -

She thinks herself beneath me—
vilifies herself as the enemy
in a form of self-sabotage.

She is not my adversary.
She is my muse.

- The Cure -

Protecting something so sacred
won't let it cross the line.
If it comes her way, she'll save it.

She's a keeper.

- The Cure -

It's hard to answer
'just friends'
as if we aren't
the most
soul-crushing,
room-dividing,
heart-healing,
life-changing
friends
you've ever met.

She is my twin flame.

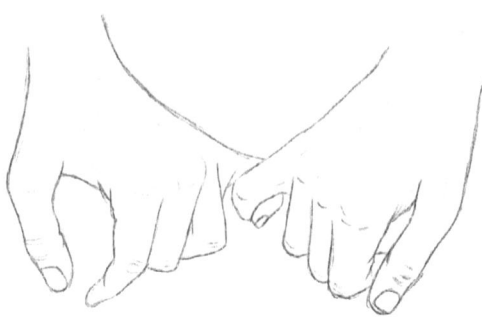

- The Cure -

When sunflowers can no longer find the sun,
they face each other.

When we can no longer find the sun,
we face each other.

- The Cure -

I know writing my feelings down
is what makes them powerful,
but my words leave me exposed.

I can't hide
if I can't lie.

If this book is open,
then so am I.

- The Cure -

I gave her words on a page.
She rearranged the sequence
and made for me
a rendition
that explained
the purpose of living—

I've never understood something so easily.

- The Cure -

How can I be disappointed
when the life I fabricated
doesn't materialise
in front of me?

I keep reading to the end,
hoping to find you
in the epilogue,
forgetting
it concludes the same way
no matter how many times
I try to rewrite it.

This book has two authors.

- The Cure -

There's no fucking way
I'd let this book end with dejection,
so hold my hand,
kiss me in the water—
this isn't a rejection.

It's a proposal
to something more
than a co-inhabitant
of the bedroom.

An invitation—
wait, no—
I'm begging:
will you be my best friend?

Let's skate through life
and see each other
on sunset nights,
because I mean it when I say
I need you by my side.

And maybe in the next,
I'm reincarnated
as your wife.

Finis coronat opus